Dare
TO BE

a COURAGEOUS GiRL

Dare
TO BE

a COURAGEOUS
GiRL

A Devotional Journal for
**Extraordinary Girls
Growing in Faith**

MARILEE PARRISH

SHILOH kidz
An Imprint of Barbour Publishing, Inc.

Published by Shiloh Kidz, an imprint of Barbour Publishing, 1810 Barbour Drive, Uhrichsville, Ohio 44683, www.shilohkidz.com

Our mission is to inspire the world with the life-changing message of the Bible.

Printed in China.

000443   1020   HA

CONTENTS

Dare!

...TO LOVE YOUR NEIGHBOR

*"You must love your neighbor
as you love yourself."*

Matthew 22:39

When Jesus said we must love our neighbors, He was not just talking about the people who live next to us—He was talking about *all* the people. Our neighbors are the people we "do life" with. And God wants us to love each one of them unconditionally.

The next time you read a verse about your neighbor, remember it's not just talking about the lady next door!

....

....

....

....

....

....

....

....

....

....

Lord, I get it! My neighbor isn't just the guy across the street. It's not just the kids next door. My neighbors are all around me! I see them every day!

CHALLENGE

What are some ways you can show love to your neighbors this week? Make a list below, and then follow through and act on your ideas. Check them off as you complete each one.

Dare!

...TO BE KIND

Show me unfailing kindness like the
Lord's kindness as long as I live.
1 Samuel 20:14 NIV

Kindness comes easily to some people. But sometimes kindness can be difficult when we are angry or upset about something. But did you know that kindness is a fruit of the Spirit? That means that God can grow more kindness in your heart as you follow Him. So the next time you feel like getting angry or lashing out at someone, take a deep breath and ask Jesus to help the fruit of kindness grow bigger in your heart.

....

....

....

....

....

....

....

....

....

....

Jesus, please help me to remember to stop and pray when I'm upset. Please grow the fruit of kindness bigger and bigger in my heart.

CHALLENGE

Ask God to bring certain people to your mind who could use an extra dose of kindness in their lives right now. Write down their names. Brainstorm ideas of how you can show kindness to those people.

Dare!

. . .TO KNOW GOD'S VOICE

*"My sheep hear My voice and I know them. They follow Me.
I give them life that lasts forever. They will never be punished.
No one is able to take them out of My hand."*

JOHN 10:27–28

Did you know that God wants to speak to you? He cares about every little thing in your life and wants to give you direction and let you know He cares. A relationship with Jesus means that you communicate with Him, and He with you. As you begin learning how to hear God's voice, you'll find that when God speaks to you, His direction will always line up with His words in the Bible. But He doesn't only speak to us through the Bible. He speaks through songs, other people, His creation—and more!

....

....

....

....

....

....

....

....

....

....

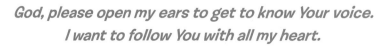

God, please open my ears to get to know Your voice.
I want to follow You with all my heart.

CHALLENGE

Think of the last time you heard God speak to you. What did He tell you? Get in the habit of writing down everything you hear from God, and ask Him to let you know for sure that it was from Him. If you are not sure if something is from your imagination or if it is from God, simply ask God to make His way clear to you, and He will—over and over again!

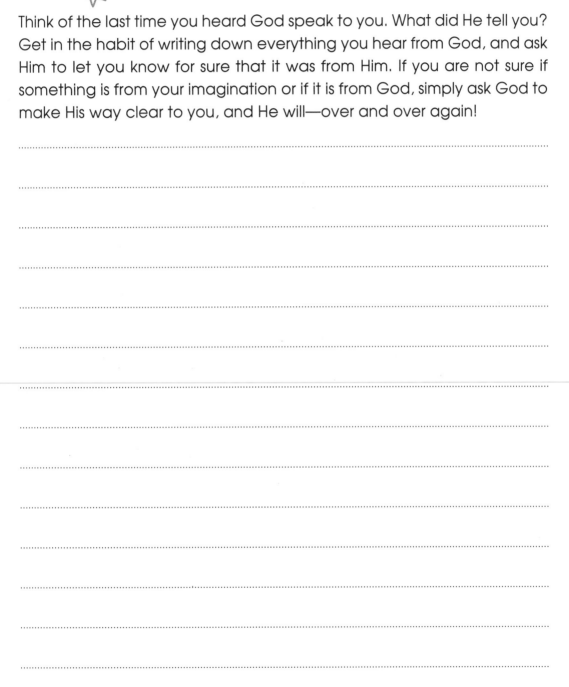

Dare!

...TO BE THANKFUL

*Always give thanks for all things to God
the Father in the name of our Lord Jesus Christ.*

Ephesians 5:20

God wants us to be thankful. And we all have plenty to be thankful for if we're on the lookout for it—even when we feel like things are going wrong. When we obey God by being thankful and not worrying, He gives us true and lasting peace. But it doesn't stay like that forever! We have to keep giving our worries to God and replacing them with thankfulness every single day. It's definitely not just a onetime thing.

....

....

....

....

....

....

....

....

....

....

Lord, I'm truly thankful for all the blessings in my life.
Help me bring my worries to You and leave them there.
I trust You and want to obey You by being thankful.

CHALLENGE

Write down one hundred things you are thankful for! If you can easily come up with one hundred, keep going! Talk to God as you make your list, thanking Him for blessing you in so many ways.

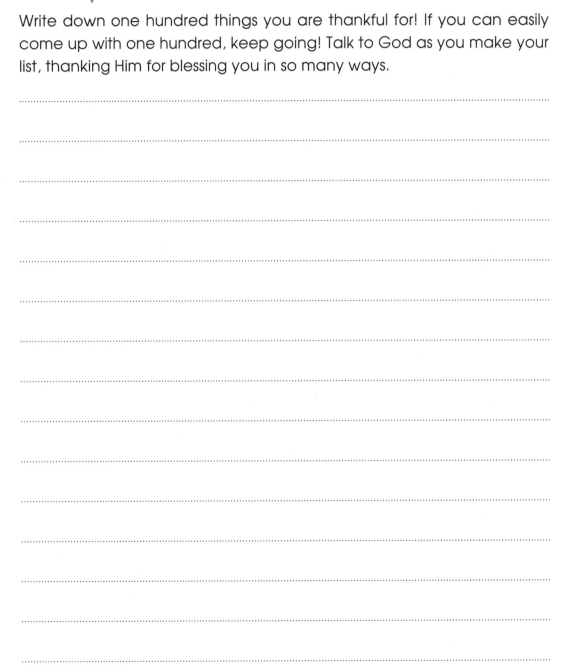

Dare!

. . .TO BE COURAGEOUS

"Be strong and have strength of heart. Do not be afraid or shake with fear because of them. For the Lord your God is the One Who goes with you. He will be faithful to you. He will not leave you alone."

Deuteronomy 31:6

Have you ever felt alone? Like no one was on your side? Or that you had to face something all by yourself? The truth is that you are never alone! God says He is with you always and He will never leave you alone. His Spirit is alive inside you, giving you strength and courage to face anything. Even when you're by yourself at bedtime, you are never truly alone. Can you take a minute and picture this? What is God showing you?

....

....

....

....

....

....

....

....

....

....

God, thank You for reminding me that I'm never alone and that You give me courage and strength to tackle anything.

CHALLENGE

Write down a few things that scare you. Maybe it's getting up in front of the classroom for a presentation or singing a solo for the concert. Ask God to give you some ideas that will help you have courage in those specific situations. Memorizing Deuteronomy 31:6 and saying it in your head before the event could be helpful. Write the verse down to help it stick in your head.

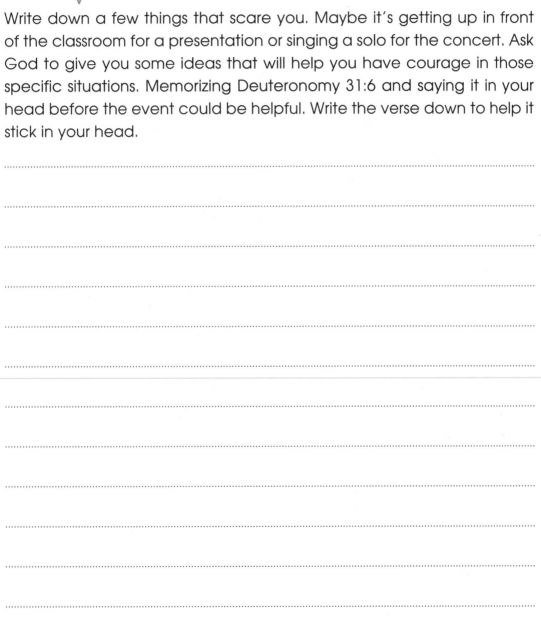

Dare!

. . .TO BE HEALTHY

*Do you not know that your body is a house of God
where the Holy Spirit lives? God gave you His Holy Spirit.
Now you belong to God. You do not belong to yourselves.*

1 Corinthians 6:19

The Bible says that your body is God's very own house! How amazing is that? God makes His home right in your body. So it is important to take care of that house, right? You can do that by eating healthy and making sure to get exercise. God doesn't leave you to take care of your body all by yourself. He lives inside you and will help if you let Him.

....

....

....

....

....

....

....

....

....

....

Lord, thanks for helping me keep Your home
healthy and clean. I'm so thankful I don't have
to figure out how to do that on my own.

CHALLENGE

List ways that you can take care of the house of God, your very own body! Think of foods that you can eat and ways to move that can help your body stay healthy and active.

....

....

....

....

....

....

....

....

....

....

....

....

Dare!

. . .TO LET GOD CHANGE YOU

*This has become my way of life: When I want to do what
is right, I always do what is wrong. My mind and heart
agree with the Law of God. But there is a different law at
work deep inside of me that fights with my mind. This law
of sin holds me in its power because sin is still in me.*

Romans 7:21–23

Does today's scripture verse sound familiar to you? You've decided that you'll never do something again, and then you find yourself doing that very same thing—again. When you find yourself repeating the same sin, take your problem straight to God. Confess your sin and tell God how you feel. Ask Him to take control of your life, and allow His Holy Spirit to change you.

_____

_____

_____

_____

_____

_____

_____

_____

_____

_____

_____

God, I want to do Your will. I'm not getting some
things right, and I need Your help. Please fill
me with Your Spirit and change my heart.

CHALLENGE

Is there something you keep failing at again and again? Is there a sin you need to confess and ask God for help in overcoming? Do so here.

Dare!

. . .TO BELIEVE

"You will know the truth and the
truth will make you free."

JOHN 8:32

God wants you to know the truth about who you are and who He is. He very much wants you to believe that truth and live like you believe it. Here's what He says about you:

- You are free and clean in the blood of Christ (Galatians 5:1; 1 John 1:7).
- He has rescued you from darkness and has brought you into His kingdom (Colossians 1:13).
- You are a precious child of the Father (John 1:12; Galatians 3:26).
- You are a friend of Christ (John 15:15).
- Nothing can separate you from God's love (Romans 8:38–39).

....

....

....

....

....

....

....

....

....

....

God, I choose to believe Your truth.
Help me live my life for You.

CHALLENGE

Look up each scripture reference from the previous page, and write it in your own words (example: "I am free and clean because Jesus died for me on the cross"). Ask Jesus to help you believe these words as you read them out loud.

Dare!

. . .TO BELONG

He gave the right and the power to become children
of God to those who received Him. He gave this
to those who put their trust in His name.

JOHN 1:12

Once you know and believe who God is and who you are because of Him, everything changes. You are free to live the life God created you to live no matter what is going on around you. You belong because God says you belong. You can love and be loved no matter what. If you end up sitting by yourself, use that time to thank God for your blessings and pray over other people in the room. This takes a lot of courage. But good news—God is with you wherever you are!

....

....

....

....

....

....

....

....

....

....

God, thank You for showing me that
I belong because You say I do!

CHALLENGE

Think about the last time you felt like you didn't belong. What made you feel that way? How can the truth of knowing that God says you belong help in situations like that in the future? Picture yourself walking into a place where you don't know many people. Instead of worrying about what other people think of you, what can you do to remind yourself that you belong? How can you help other people feel like they belong too?

Dare!

...TO HELP OTHERS KNOW THE TRUTH

Christ made us free. Stay that way.

GALATIANS 5:1

God made you to be free! He wants you to be free to be your courageous self in every situation. And that frees you up to share that truth with others. Your job as a Jesus follower is to love the people around you. As you love those around you and build friendships, you can share the amazing message of God's love and freedom by the way you live.

Jesus, it's amazing to think that I became part of Your body when You called me and I responded by giving my life to You. Help me to have the courage to share this message with the people in my life.

CHALLENGE

Most people feel like they don't belong. They don't know the truth about God and who He says they are. Think of ways to help other people feel that they belong. When you see someone looking alone and uncomfortable, how can you help? Make a list of ideas. Pray over this list and ask God for courage to carry out your ideas.

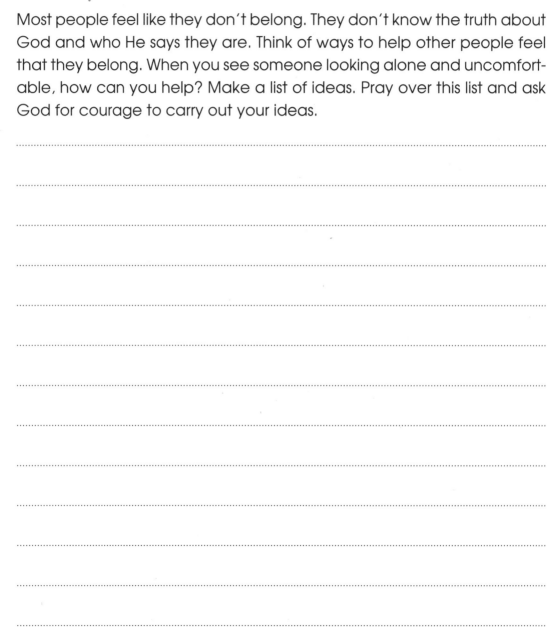

Dare!

. . .TO WORSHIP

Give to the Lord the honor that belongs to Him.
Worship the Lord in the beauty of holy living.

PSALM 29:2

What comes to mind when you think of the word *worship*? Worship isn't just about going to church on Sunday and singing some songs. Worship is the way you live your life to show that you love God. It can include singing and prayer. But did you know that you can be worshipping God while you clean your room or rake your grandma's yard? Anything you do out of love for God and others can be an act of worship.

I love You, Lord. I want to worship You and live my life in a way that makes Your heart happy. Teach me how to worship.

CHALLENGE

Make a list of the ways that you can show your love to God. What makes God's heart happy? Write God a love letter.

Dare!

...TO BE FREE

"Come to Me, all of you who work and have heavy loads. I will give you rest. Follow My teachings and learn from Me. I am gentle and do not have pride. You will have rest for your souls. For My way of carrying a load is easy and My load is not heavy."

Matthew 11:28–30

Jesus wants you to come to Him about every single thing. He wants to share your whole life with you—the good, the bad, the easy and fun, the difficult and heavy. He offers to give your soul a rest. A deep soul rest is the kind you need when you're really tired from trying to make everyone happy. Living freely and lightly sounds pretty good, right? So come to Jesus. Bring Him all your thoughts and feelings.

....

....

....

....

....

....

....

....

....

....

....

....

Jesus, I want to share my whole life with You. Show me how to live freely and lightly without trying to please everyone else.

CHALLENGE

Look up Matthew 11:28–30 in The Message translation of the Bible. You can find it online at Biblegateway.com. How do these verses make you feel? What do you need to bring to Jesus today?

....

....

....

....

....

....

....

....

....

....

....

....

Dare!

. . .TO SERVE

"For I was hungry and you gave Me food to eat.
I was thirsty and you gave Me water to drink.
I was a stranger and you gave Me a room."

MATTHEW 25:35

Serving someone else means that you put that person's needs above your own; you find out what they need and do your best to help them. Did you know that when you serve others you are actually serving Jesus? Jesus said in Matthew 25:40 (NIV), "Truly I tell you, whatever you did for one of the least of these brothers and sisters of mine, you did for me." Wow! That changes things a bit, doesn't it?

....

....

....

....

....

....

....

....

....

....

Jesus, I want to help take care of needs in my community. Give me a heart to serve others, knowing that I'm really serving You!

CHALLENGE

Write down some ways you can serve at church or get involved with needy people in your community. Go over this list with your family. How can you all get involved together? Most communities have a soup kitchen, and many churches stock up on supplies to help people in need. Find out how you can help, and remember that you're serving Jesus as you do it!

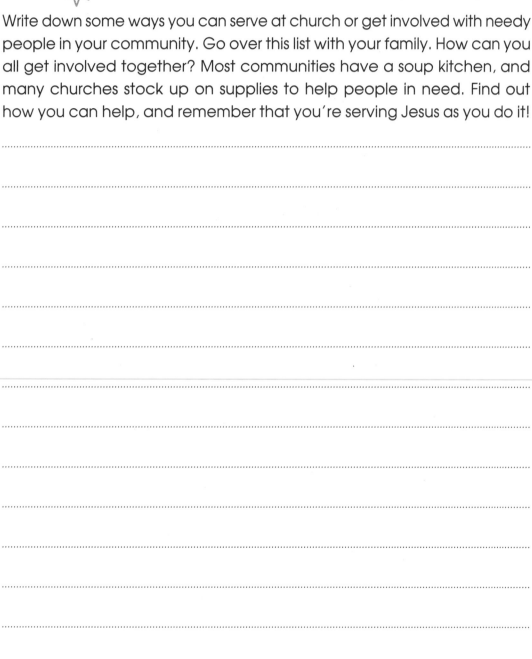

Dare!

. . .TO KEEP GOING

The Lord will finish the work He started for me.
O Lord, Your loving-kindness lasts forever.
Do not turn away from the works of Your hands.

PSALM 138:8

You were put on this earth for a purpose. You didn't happen by accident, and the Bible tells us that God knows the number of your days and the number of hairs on your head. God started a good work in you the day you were born. He has great plans for your life and wants to be with you every step of the way. Seek Him for every decision, big or small. He wants to walk with you through them all.

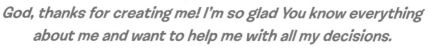

God, thanks for creating me! I'm so glad You know everything about me and want to help me with all my decisions.

CHALLENGE

Look up Philippians 1:6 and Jeremiah 29:11–13. Rewrite them in your own words. How do these verses apply to you specifically?

Dare!

. . .TO RUN FROM SIN

Turn away from what is sinful. Do what is good. Look for peace and follow it. The eyes of the Lord are on those who do what is right and good. His ears are open to their cry.

PSALM 34:14–15

The Bible tells us that we need to turn away from evil—to actually stop and go the other direction. Run! We can't just assume that trouble won't find us if we're not looking for it. Our enemy the devil is constantly looking for ways to get us to turn away from God and destroy our peace. Ask God to help you turn and go the other way so you can keep your eyes on Jesus.

....

....

....

....

....

....

....

....

....

....

....

God, please help me to run from sin and to seek You in all things. When I'm tempted to do the wrong thing, remind me that You have given me the power to make good choices.

CHALLENGE

Ask Jesus to show you anything in your heart right now that you need to bring to Him. Is there a sin in your life that you need to confess? It feels really good to get it off your chest and hand it over to Jesus for Him to help.

....

....

....

....

....

....

....

....

....

....

....

....

Dare!

...TO LIVE UPSIDE DOWN

"The person who is not trying to honor himself will be made important."

Matthew 23:12

A lot of Jesus' words seem upside down from what most people believe. Jesus says that we love others by serving them. The first shall be last, and the last shall be first. Being great comes from serving others. But too many kids are worried about how many "likes" they can get online and don't care much about anything or anyone else. Here comes the upside-down truth: Jesus says that the person who is *not* trying to get the most attention will be made important.

....

....

....

....

....

....

....

....

....

....

Jesus, please forgive me when I worry about how many people like me. I want to find joy in serving You and others.

CHALLENGE

Do you think the kids scrambling to get a lot of "likes" are living the life Jesus wants for them? Why or why not? What would living an upside-down life look like for you? Write down anything that comes to mind.

Dare!

. . .TO TELL YOUR STORY

"It must be preached that men must be sorry for their sins and turn from them. Then they will be forgiven. This must be preached in His name to all nations beginning in Jerusalem. You are to tell what you have seen."

Luke 24:47–48

Jesus wants us to tell others about what we've seen Him do. He told the disciples to tell everyone about everything they saw and heard from Jesus. He wants us to share what He is doing in our lives too. People want to know that a friendship with Jesus makes a difference in their lives. Telling this to others is called sharing your testimony. A testimony is your personal story about Jesus and what you've seen Him do in your life.

....

....

....

....

....

....

....

....

....

....

Jesus, thank You for all the amazing things You've done in my life. Use my story to bring other people to know You.

CHALLENGE

Take some time and write down what you've been praying for and how God has answered you. How has Jesus changed your life? Write down how you first came to know Jesus and what He has been doing in your life since then. Your testimony about Jesus is powerful and important.

....

....

....

....

....

....

....

....

....

....

....

....

Dare!

. . .TO SEARCH FOR TRUTH

Dear Christian friends, do not believe every spirit.
But test the spirits to see if they are from God for
there are many false preachers in the world.

1 JOHN 4:1

Always comparing what people say about God with His Word is important. Some people think certain things they believe are in the Bible, but they really aren't. Sometimes even people you trust can say things that aren't true about God. So look it up for yourself. You have the Spirit of God right there in your heart to teach you, so if someone says something about God and it doesn't quite feel right, check it out.

....

....

....

....

....

....

....

....

....

....

....

God, please give me wisdom about You.
Thank You that I have Your Spirit to guide me.

CHALLENGE

The Message translation of 1 John 4:1 says, "Don't believe everything you hear. Carefully weigh and examine what people tell you. Not everyone who talks about God comes from God." Is there anything you've heard about God from your friends or other people that doesn't seem quite right? Journal about it here. Then look up what the Bible really says and write down the truth.

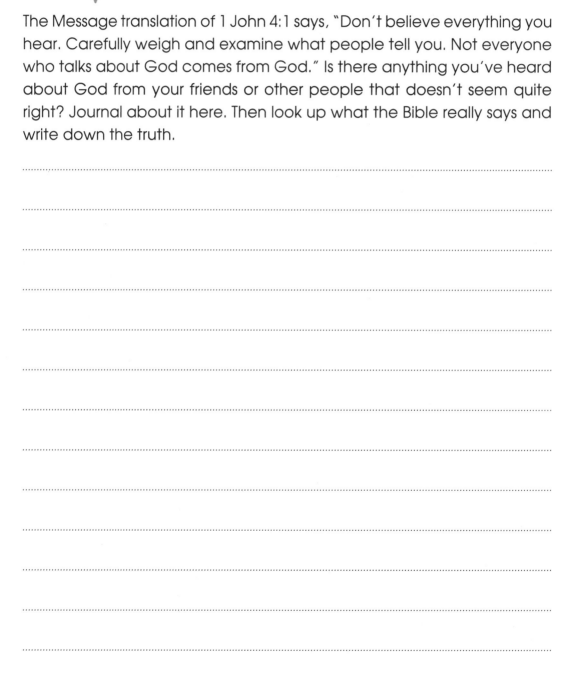

Dare!

. . .TO LOVE GOD

God has shown His love to us by sending His only Son into the world. God did this so we might have life through Christ. This is love! It is not that we loved God but that He loved us. For God sent His Son to pay for our sins with His own blood.

1 JOHN 4:9–10

Sometimes it's hard to know how to love God back because His gift of giving His only Son's life to show us how much He loves us is so great. His vast love can be overwhelming! But we can show our love to God by loving others, following His Word, and listening for His voice and obeying what He says. He is the Author of love, and He'll continue to show us how to love better and better as we follow Him.

....

....

....

....

....

....

....

....

....

....

God, please help me to listen for Your voice in my life and to follow after You, relying on the love You have for me.

CHALLENGE

Look up John 14:21–24. What does this passage say about how we show love to God? Journal about what this means to you.

Dare!

. . .TO FIND A MENTOR

Let us help each other to love others and to do good. Let us not stay away from church meetings. Some people are doing this all the time. Comfort each other as you see the day of His return coming near.

HEBREWS 10:24–25

Do you know what a mentor is? It's someone who is usually older than you who loves God and is willing to teach you some things about being a follower of Jesus. A mentor needs to be a safe person your parents know about. This person should be dependable so that you can plan on meeting together a few times a month to talk about God and pray together. Pray for God to direct you to someone who can encourage you and help you grow in your faith.

Lord, please direct me to a wise
mentor who can help me grow in You.

CHALLENGE

Is finding a mentor something you might like to do to get closer to God? Make a list with your parents of several Jesus-following people who come to mind. Then give them a call and set up your first get-together.

Dare!

...TO HAVE FAITH

"For sure, I tell you, if you have faith as a mustard seed,
you will say to this mountain, 'Move from here to over there,'
and it would move over. You will be able to do anything."

Matthew 17:20

67

The disciples were having a hard time getting a job done. They weren't so sure about this new power that Jesus had given them. Jesus reminded them that it was the power of God working inside them that gave them the ability to get the job done, not their own power. The same is true for you. Jesus reminded His followers about mustard-seed faith. Mustard seeds are super tiny but grow into trees. When you have small faith in a huge God, anything is possible!

....

....

....

....

....

....

....

....

....

*Jesus, help me trust You to be faithful and all-powerful
in my life. Though my faith is small sometimes,
I know that Your power is big!*

CHALLENGE

Do you believe that Jesus is all-powerful and can do anything? Is there anything in your life right now that feels too big or too small for God? Write down what you're thinking about. Ask Jesus to help you see things through His eyes.

....

....

....

....

....

....

....

....

....

....

Dare!

. . .TO BE GENEROUS

"Do not gather together for yourself riches of this earth. They will be eaten by bugs and become rusted. Men can break in and steal them. Gather together riches in heaven where they will not be eaten by bugs or become rusted. Men cannot break in and steal them. For wherever your riches are, your heart will be there also."

MATTHEW 6:19–21

As you grow up, you'll see more and more that most people chase after things that don't last—money, clothes, electronics, and more. But here's the truth: chasing after those kinds of things will never fill you up and make you truly happy. Only God can meet the deep longings in your heart, and He wants you to share what you've been given with others.

....

....

....

....

....

....

....

....

....

....

Lord, please give me a generous heart to think of others and their needs before my own. Show me how to help the people around me who need something.

CHALLENGE

Think of your community. Can you think of any specific needs of the people who live around you or go to your church? Write those down. Ask God to show you how you can help.

....

....

....

....

....

....

....

....

....

....

....

....

Dare!

. . .TO KNOW JESUS

"These people show respect to Me with their mouth, but their heart is far from Me. Their worship of Me is worth nothing. They teach what men have made up."

Matthew 15:8–9

The Pharisees in Jesus' day knew a lot about God and all the Old Testament laws. In fact, they prided themselves on looking good on the outside and following all the laws strictly. They thought they knew everything about God, but they were actually very far from Him. People can say a lot of things, but it's what's inside their hearts that really matters. Remember that actions always speak louder than words.

....

....

....

....

....

....

....

....

....

....

....

Jesus, I want to know the real You. Bless our friendship and remind me that You want to have conversations with me all day long.

CHALLENGE

Following Jesus doesn't mean following all the rules and never messing up. Following Jesus means you have a real friendship with Him in which you learn His Word and talk *with* Him about it. You get to know His heart and His love for you. You love Him back and you share that love with others. Do you feel like you have a good friendship with Jesus? List some ways that you could become better friends with Him.

....

....

....

....

....

....

....

....

....

....

Dare!

. . .TO LOOK FOR THE WAY OUT

*You have never been tempted to sin in any different way
than other people. God is faithful. He will not allow you to be
tempted more than you can take. But when you are tempted,
He will make a way for you to keep from falling into sin.*

1 Corinthians 10:13

Our enemy is out to trip up kids in any way he can. Telling you that you're not cool if you don't play the most popular video games, urging you to look at something online that you know you shouldn't look at, convincing you to tell lies to get out of trouble—those are all tricks from hell. Don't fall for them! Instead, ask God to fill you up with His power to overcome all the tricks of the enemy.

God, please help me to look for the way out every time I'm tempted to do the wrong thing.

CHALLENGE

First Corinthians 10:13 in the New International Version says, "When you are tempted, he will also provide a way out so that you can endure it." Write this verse again in your journal here. Writing it down will help you remember it. Ask the Holy Spirit to help you memorize it and bring it to mind anytime you feel tempted to do the wrong thing.

Dare!

. . .TO FOLLOW THE LEADER

As He saw many people, He had loving-pity on them.
They were troubled and were walking around everywhere.
They were like sheep without a shepherd.

MATTHEW 9:36

When Jesus came to earth, He saw that the people were acting like sheep that followed whatever the leader was doing—even if it was a bad idea. The Bible says that Jesus had compassion for these people. He knew what caused them to make those choices. He loved them and wanted to help. He came to be the Good Shepherd, to lead people to Himself. He showed how to love and to serve others with kindness and respect.

....

....

....

....

....

....

....

....

....

....

....

Jesus, thank You for showing me how to be a good leader.
Help me to lead others well as I follow You.

CHALLENGE

Do you consider yourself a leader or a follower? What do you base that judgment on? Ask Jesus what He wants you to know about that position. What do you hear Him saying to you?

Dare!

. . .TO WATCH YOUR TALK

Watch your talk! No bad words should be coming from your mouth. Say what is good. Your words should help others grow as Christians.

EPHESIANS 4:29

Words can either build people up or tear them down. Every time you speak to someone, you can leave them feeling better or worse about themselves. You can encourage them and help them feel like they are valuable and can do great things in life, or you can discourage them and leave them with bad thoughts. Pray for God to help you speak words that encourage others in a way that points them to the love of Jesus.

....

....

....

....

....

....

....

....

....

....

God, please help me to build other people up and
encourage them with my words. I want to leave
them feeling loved, encouraged, and hopeful.

CHALLENGE

Have you been affected by other people's words? Write down some good things people have said to you. Now write down some negative things people have said to you. Can you forgive those people and let those words go? Ask Jesus for help. What kind words can you share with others?

Dare!

. . .TO KNOW GOD'S WORD

"So My Word which goes from My mouth will not return to Me empty. It will do what I want it to do, and will carry out My plan well."

Isaiah 55:11

Your Bible is an amazing tool from God. Inside it holds wonders, mysteries, miracles, adventures—and it's all true! But here is the most amazing thing: it is *alive*! Did you know that? God's Word is alive. The Bible tells us in Hebrews 4:12 that God's Word is living and active! God's Word is how we get to know the truth about who God is and what He has done. It's how we begin to hear God's voice.

....

....

....

....

....

....

....

....

....

....

God, thank You for loving us so much that You gave
us an instruction manual to help us through life.

CHALLENGE

The Holy Spirit uses words from the Bible to teach us God's will. And when you hide God's Word in your heart, you learn how to live a full and God-honoring life. How can you hide God's Word in your heart? List some ideas.

Dare!

...TO BE WHO GOD MADE YOU TO BE

For God did not give us a spirit of fear. He gave us a spirit of power and of love and of a good mind.

2 Timothy 1:7

God has given each of us different personalities, and there is nothing wrong, and everything right, with the way that God made you! He made some kids outgoing, some curious, some creative, and some organized and neat. However He made you, He wants you to use that personality to honor Him. You never ever have to be afraid of what other people might say or think about you. He made you the way you are on purpose. Only God's opinion of you really matters.

....

....

....

....

....

....

....

....

....

....

God, thank You for my personality. You designed me to think and act a special way. Help me to honor You with my thoughts and actions.

CHALLENGE

Make a list of your personality traits. What do you like and dislike? Are you shy or outgoing? Go through your list and thank God for making you the way you are.

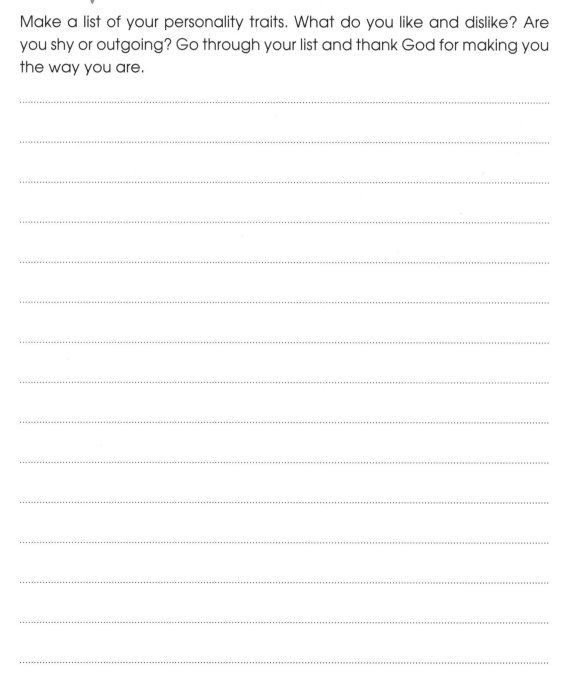

Dare!

. . .TO BE LOVED

*"You are of great worth in My eyes. You are honored
and I love you. I will give other men in your place.
I will trade other people for your life."*

Isaiah 43:4

The Message translation of the Bible says Isaiah 43:3–4 this way: "I am GOD, your personal God, The Holy of Israel, your Savior. I paid a huge price for you. . . . That's how much you mean to me! That's how much I love you! I'd sell off the whole world to get you back, trade the creation just for you."

You are of great worth to God. He would trade the whole world to get you back! He is your own personal Savior, with you always. God wants your friends and family to know this great love too.

....

....

....

....

....

....

....

....

....

....

Thank You for Your amazing love for us, God.

CHALLENGE

List your friends and family members who seem far from God or don't know that God loves them. How does God want you to share this amazing love with them? Talk to Him about this. Ask Him for courage to share His love with others.

Dare!

. . .TO GROW SPIRITUALLY

"Do not work for food that does not last. Work for food that lasts forever. The Son of Man will give you that kind of food. God the Father has shown He will do this."

JOHN 6:27

Jesus' followers saw Him multiply the loaves and fishes to feed thousands. Jesus had given them all a free meal, and they knew He could do it again. They were hungry, so they went to find Him.

They weren't necessarily coming to hear what Jesus had to say. They wanted something for nothing. But Jesus told them not to come just so He could fill their stomach with food, but to come and listen so that their hearts would be filled with life.

....

....

....

....

....

....

....

....

....

....

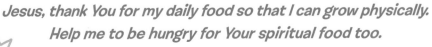

Jesus, thank You for my daily food so that I can grow physically.
Help me to be hungry for Your spiritual food too.

CHALLENGE

Just as we need to eat every day to live and grow, we need to have Jesus and His Word in us every day so that we can live and grow spiritually. What are some ways that you can grow spiritually? List your ideas here.

....

....

....

....

....

....

....

....

....

....

....

....

Dare!

. . .TO BRING HOPE

The Spirit of the Lord God is on me, because the Lord has chosen me to bring good news to poor people. He has sent me to heal those with a sad heart. He has sent me to tell those who are being held and those in prison that they can go free.

Isaiah 61:1

Jesus came to heal people with hurting hearts and to set people free. He wasn't just talking about physical conditions like people who need healing from an illness or who need to be set free from prison. He was talking about people with broken hearts and those held captive by fear. Jesus came to bring hope to anyone who needs it, and He loves to comfort people. Did you know that He can use you to help comfort hurting people too? The smile of a child can do wonders for some people.

Jesus, please show me how I can help hurting people.
Please give me courage to help bring hope to others.

CHALLENGE

Have you ever felt sad or hopeless? Write down how you felt at that time. This will help you to have compassion for others going through hard times. Do you know anyone with a broken heart? Jot down a few names. Ask Jesus to show you how He can use you to bring hope to those hurting people. He'll point you in the right direction and give you courage as you go.

. . .TO GO TO GOD

*But the wisdom that comes from heaven is first of all pure.
Then it gives peace. It is gentle and willing to obey. It is
full of loving-kindness and of doing good. It has no doubts
and does not pretend to be something it is not.*

JAMES 3:17

Lots of people head straight to Google whenever they have a question. But heavenly wisdom is hard to find there. You might eventually find the answer you're looking for, but it will be mixed with thousands of other opinions, and you have to sift through a bunch of junk to find some truth. The Bible tells us that when we need wisdom, we can ask God for it and He'll give it to us—just because we asked Him (James 1:5)!

God, I definitely need lots of wisdom in this mixed-up world. Please give me the desire to come to You for the answers to all my questions.

CHALLENGE

What are some questions you have in your life right now? Are you struggling with a friendship or a specific class in school? Write down any problems you are facing. Ask Jesus to give you wisdom from His Word. Then look up answers in your Bible. Ask a trusted, believing adult for help on how to find these answers in your Bible. Write down anything God tells you.

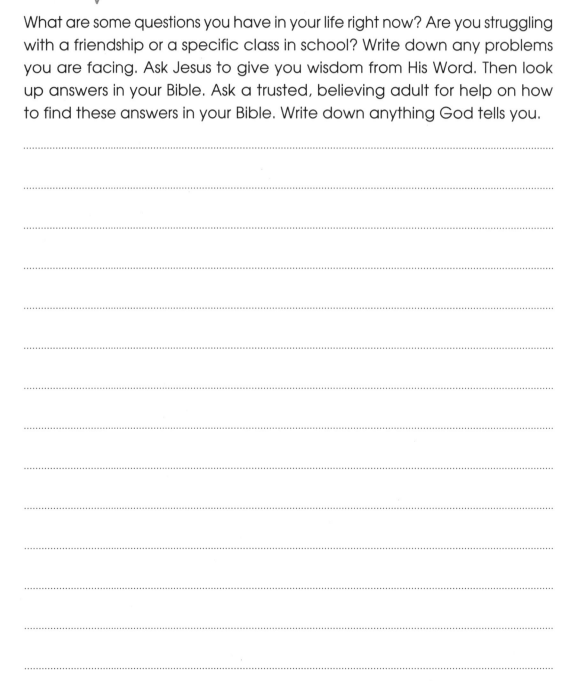

Dare!

. . .TO GIVE YOUR BEST

Whatever work you do, do it with all your heart. Do it for the Lord and not for men. Remember that you will get your reward from the Lord. He will give you what you should receive. You are working for the Lord Christ.

COLOSSIANS 3:23–24

Remember that even homework and chores can be an act of worship to God. God sees you as you clean your room and do your chores at home. He cares about everything you're doing. So whatever you are doing, work at it with all your heart. Pray for Him to give you joy in serving and helping around the house (turning worship music on while you work always helps too!). When you realize you're actually serving and worshipping God as you work, you become a joy to your parents and teachers too.

Lord, help me do all my work with joy,
knowing I'm really serving You.

CHALLENGE

Are there any specific chores or schoolwork that you have a hard time doing with joy? Journal about them here. Would you maybe work a bit differently if you had to hand your homework straight to Jesus? Imagine Jesus working right beside you as you do chores or other work. Ask Him for help in seeing that Jesus is the One you are actually serving as you work.

Dare!

. . .TO NEVER GIVE UP

If a man does things to please the Holy Spirit, he will have life that lasts forever. Do not let yourselves get tired of doing good. If we do not give up, we will get what is coming to us at the right time.

GALATIANS 6:8–9

Jesus tells a story of a very persistent woman in Luke 18:1–8. Persistent means that she never gave up. And she was rewarded for that! Quitters give up because they've run out of their own strength. They have nothing left to give, so they give up in defeat. But followers of Jesus depend on His strength. Remember that His power shines through in our weakness. Keep coming back to God every day in prayer. Be persistent. Don't give up.

....

....

....

....

....

....

....

....

....

....

Lord, thank You that I don't have to depend on my own strength. I'd much rather count on Yours instead.

CHALLENGE

Read the story of the persistent woman in Luke 18:1–8. Ask Jesus what He wants you to notice in this story. Write down what you hear from God. Then invite Him to give you power through His Spirit who is alive in you so that you can depend on His strength when you feel like giving up.

Dare!

...TO THINK GOOD THOUGHTS

Keep your minds thinking about whatever is true, whatever is respected, whatever is right, whatever is pure, whatever can be loved, and whatever is well thought of. If there is anything good and worth giving thanks for, think about these things.

Philippians 4:8

Our thoughts can get us in lots and lots of trouble. It's easy to get off track and think about things we shouldn't—even when we're praying! The next time you find yourself thinking about something that isn't right, ask Jesus to step right into your thoughts and change them! Just speak His name and ask Him to come to your rescue. He can change the direction of your thoughts and turn them into thoughts and actions that are pure and true and lovely.

....

....

....

....

....

....

....

....

....

....

Jesus, Your name is powerful. I pray You will step in and change my thoughts to be pure and true when I'm distracted.

CHALLENGE

On this page, write down the things you want to talk about with God today. List any specific prayer requests. This will help you stay on track as you pray. Make sure to take some time to do some listening as you pray too. Remember, prayer is a conversation! Write down anything God tells you.

Dare!

. . . TO FORGIVE

You must be kind to each other. Think of the other person. Forgive other people just as God forgave you because of Christ's death on the cross.

Ephesians 4:32

Jesus' death on the cross paid for all our sins once and for all. We still ask forgiveness from God when we sin, because sin gets in the way of our friendship with Him. When we come to Him and confess our sins (telling Him we're sorry about what we've done), our friendship with God gets fixed quickly. God wants us to forgive others just as quickly, because when we carry around unforgiveness, it keeps getting in the way of everything.

Lord, help me to forgive Your way: quickly and completely. Thank You for Your death on the cross that paid for my sins forever.

CHALLENGE

Are there friends or family members who have hurt you recently? List them here. Ask God for help to forgive them. Have you hurt someone's feelings yourself? Write down that person's name. Go to that person and tell them you're sorry. Write them a letter if you have trouble saying these kinds of things out loud. Ask God for the courage to do the right thing.

Dare!

. . .TO STAY ALERT

*Keep awake! Watch at all times. The devil is working
against you. He is walking around like a hungry lion
with his mouth open. He is looking for someone to eat.
Stand against him and be strong in your faith.*

1 Peter 5:8–9

Even though the devil knows he has already been defeated by Jesus, he is still trying his best to get into your head and discourage you so you won't be able to live well for Jesus. That's why Jesus wants you to stay alert. Don't fall for Satan's tricks! As a child of God, you have power in the name of Jesus to get rid of any evil you come up against. You don't have to be afraid, just alert. Jesus is always with you to help!

....

....

....

....

....

....

....

....

....

....

....

Lord, help me to stay alert and not
fall for any of the enemy's tricks.

CHALLENGE

James 4:7 in the Amplified Bible says, "Submit to (the authority of) God. Resist the devil (stand firm against him) and he will flee from you." What pictures do you see in your imagination as you read this verse? Draw them here.

Dare!

...TO BE WISE WITH YOUR SCREENS

Be careful how you live. Live as men who are wise and not foolish. Make the best use of your time. These are sinful days. Do not be foolish. Understand what the Lord wants you to do.

EPHESIANS 5:15–17

Look around at any time of day and you will see just about everyone looking at a screen. There are many benefits to technology and social media, but there are also a lot of negatives. Does God care about your screen time usage? You bet! Screen time and video games can easily become an idol. An idol is anything that comes before God in your life or turns your attention away from Him.

God, please help me not to put screen time ahead of You.
I don't want it to be an idol that gets in the way of my
relationship with You. Help me to be wise online.

CHALLENGE

Is there a chance you're wasting time on things God might not want you to be doing? Write down the first thing that comes to mind after reading that. Using screens and having fun online is okay as long as you are making wise choices about what you're doing and how long you're doing it. Talk to God about it. What limits have your parents set up for screen time in your house? Talk with your parents about these limits and write them down as a reminder.

....

....

....

....

....

....

....

....

....

. . .TO SHINE

Be glad you can do the things you should be doing. Do all things without arguing and talking about how you wish you did not have to do them. In that way, you can prove yourselves to be without blame. You are God's children and no one can talk against you, even in a sin-loving and sin-sick world. You are to shine as lights among the sinful people of this world.

PHILIPPIANS 2:14–15

Seems like everyone wants to be a star these days, right? Even kids make silly videos, post them on YouTube or TikTok, and become instantly famous. But Jesus wants us to be a different kind of star. You are a child of God, and He gives you all the attention you could ever want. His desire is for you to shine for Him like a star in the sky. If you live like that, you'll stand out for sure!

God, help me live a different kind of life than everyone else. Help me light up the world with Your love instead of seeking attention from others.

CHALLENGE

Read Philippians 2:14–15 again. According to this verse, how can you shine like a star, proving yourself to be without blame? What does that mean to you?

....

....

....

....

....

....

....

....

....

....

Dare!

. . .TO PRAY

Tell your sins to each other. And pray for each other
so you may be healed. The prayer from the heart
of a man right with God has much power.

JAMES 5:16

Something powerful and mysterious happens when we pray. We can't see exactly what happens in the unseen world when we pray, but we do know that our prayers matter to God and that they can accomplish a lot. God's Word tells us to pray for others so that their bodies, minds, and hearts can be restored and made whole.

....

....

....

....

....

....

....

....

....

....

....

Thank You that my prayers matter to You, God! I bring my friends and family before You and ask that You would do Your healing work in their hearts and bodies.

CHALLENGE

The New Living Translation of today's verse says, "The earnest prayer of a righteous person has great power and produces wonderful results." Who do you need to pray for? Make a list of family members with illnesses or broken hearts. Talk to God about each one and ask for His blessing on their lives.

Dare!

. . .TO BE FAITHFUL

"He that is faithful with little things is faithful with big things also. He that is not honest with little things is not honest with big things."

LUKE 16:10

Being faithful means that you do what you say you're going to do. It also means that you're trustworthy. If you're faithful in the little things like cleaning up your room when you say you're going to, your parents will trust you to be faithful in bigger things. If you always tell the truth, your family and friends will learn that you are a trustworthy person. The opposite is also true: if you lie about little things, you won't be trusted when it's really important.

God, I want to be faithful in all things—big and small.
Help me to be a trustworthy person.

CHALLENGE

What does a faithful friendship look like to you? Are you that kind of friend? Do you believe you are a faithful person? Why or why not? Write a commitment to Jesus to be more faithful. Ask for His help to keep your commitments.

....

....

....

....

....

....

....

....

....

....

....

Dare!

...TO BE DIFFERENT

It is true, we live in a body of flesh. But we do not fight like people of the world. We do not use those things to fight with that the world uses. We use the things God gives to fight with and they have power. Those things God gives to fight with destroy the strong-places of the devil.

2 Corinthians 10:3–4

As a child of God, you have been given special spiritual armor. Your spiritual armor consists of special weapons that God has given you to protect you from evil. This armor also helps you to live in this world but not be of it (see John 17:14–16). That means that you don't have the same value system as the people of the world who aren't following Jesus. Being different is good! Pray and ask God for the courage to be different as you put on your armor every day.

God, please give me the courage
to be different as I follow You.

CHALLENGE

Read Ephesians 6:10–18. Draw a picture of yourself as a soldier with your spiritual armor on. Can you picture yourself putting on the whole armor of God? Ask God for help remembering to do this every day.

Dare!

. . .TO BE A GOOD EXAMPLE

*Let no one show little respect for you because you are young.
Show other Christians how to live by your life. They should be
able to follow you in the way you talk and in what you do.
Show them how to live in faith and in love and in holy living.*

1 TIMOTHY 4:12

When God's Spirit comes and lives inside of you, He gives you, His child, the power to be an example to others—even to older people. Sometimes it takes the faith of a child to get a hardened heart to hear from God. You never know when your life will touch someone else, but you can be sure that everyone you know is watching to see if your faith is making a difference in your life.

....

....

....

....

....

....

....

....

....

God, thank You for showing me who I am in You!
Help me to be a good example to others!

CHALLENGE

Do you know who determines your value as a person? Is it your family? Your friends? Other kids at school? Nope. Only God has the right to tell you who you are! Why? Because He made you! Write a thank-you note to God for making you the way you are. Don't forget to thank Him for the special gifts and talents He gave you too! You are His princess. How can you use these truths to be a good example to others?

....

....

....

....

....

....

....

....

....

....

....

....

....

Dare!

. . .TO GROW FRUIT

But the fruit that comes from having the Holy Spirit in our lives is: love, joy, peace, not giving up, being kind, being good, having faith, being gentle, and being the boss over our own desires. The Law is not against these things.

GALATIANS 5:22–23

When the love of Jesus is firmly planted in your heart, the fruits of the Spirit begin to grow—and that's a really big deal! As the Spirit of God works in the garden of your heart, He produces spiritual fruit because of what Jesus did for you on the cross. His death and eternal life give you new life—just like a spring garden. As you continue to follow Jesus, these fruits begin to take root and grow in your heart, getting bigger and bigger until you are bursting with spiritual fruit.

God, please help Your fruits grow
bigger in the garden of my heart!

CHALLENGE

List all the fruits of the Spirit from Galatians 5:22–23. Which fruits need to grow a bit bigger in the garden of your heart? Circle them. Ask the Holy Spirit to help them grow!

Dare!

. . .TO STAY CLOSE TO JESUS

He will feed His flock like a shepherd. He will gather
the lambs in His arms and carry them close to His heart.
He will be gentle in leading those that are with young.

Isaiah 40:11

Jesus is your gentle Shepherd. Can you picture Him carrying you close to His heart? You are very important to Him, and He loves you very much. Commit to staying close to your Shepherd. He will always lead you on the right path. He will refresh and restore your life, making you strong. Pray that Jesus continues to make His voice known to you.

....

....

....

....

....

....

....

....

....

....

....

Jesus, thank You for caring for me like a gentle shepherd. I love the thought of You carrying me close to Your heart. I will follow You, Jesus. Help me to recognize You as You speak to me.

CHALLENGE

Psalm 23:1–3 says, "The Lord is my Shepherd. I will have everything I need. He lets me rest in fields of green grass. He leads me beside the quiet waters. He makes me strong again. He leads me in the way of living right with Himself which brings honor to His name." Can you draw a picture of what you see in your imagination when you read this passage?

Dare!

. . .TO BE RESPECTFUL

Your heart should be holy and set apart for the Lord God. Always be ready to tell everyone who asks you why you believe as you do. Be gentle as you speak and show respect. Keep your heart telling you that you have done what is right. If men speak against you, they will be ashamed when they see the good way you have lived as a Christian.

1 PETER 3:15–16

When you follow Jesus, people are going to wonder what makes you different. Some people will disagree with your faith in unkind ways. Don't get embarrassed or angry; simply ask for God's help. He is right there with you, and He sees everything that's happening. He wants you to answer with gentleness and respect. The reason people ask is because they are looking for hope too. And they want to know if yours is real!

God, help me remember that everyone else is looking for hope in You too. You created them that way. Help me to be gentle and respect others when I share my faith in You.

CHALLENGE

List some ways that you could share your faith with others. For example, if someone asks why you smile all the time, what would you say?

Dare!

...TO SEE OTHERS AS EQUALS

Then Peter said, "I can see, for sure, that God does not respect one person more than another. He is pleased with any man in any nation who honors Him and does what is right."

Acts 10:34–35

The Bible says that God doesn't play favorites. That means that He doesn't think one person is more important than another person because of what they do, where they live, or how much money they have. That kind of stuff doesn't matter to God. We are all equal because of Jesus. God's door is wide open for everyone no matter what kind of job they do or what kind of family they come from. The love of Jesus is for everyone!

....

....

....

....

....

....

....

....

....

God, thank You that Your door is open to everyone!
You love each of us abundantly and equally.

CHALLENGE

Can you think of several people you know who have difficult service jobs—for instance, maybe a janitor at your school or church? Take a minute and think about the kind of work they do and how hard it must be. Write down some names of people with hard jobs and list some ways that you could bless them. Who else needs to know that they are important? Write down anyone who comes to mind.

Dare!

...TO WEAR GOD'S KIND OF CLOTHES

Therefore, as God's chosen people, holy and dearly loved, clothe yourselves with compassion, kindness, humility, gentleness and patience.

COLOSSIANS 3:12 NIV

God's kind of clothes are made of love—love for God and love for others. That's what really matters! Wrapping yourself up in compassion, kindness, and patience will warm you and everyone around you too! God loves you very much, and He wants you to share His love with other people. Picking out nice clothes is fun, but putting on God's clothes is the first step. So, the next time you're headed out, reach for God's kind of clothes, and you'll be ready for anything.

....

....

....

....

....

....

....

....

....

....

God, help me to wear things that make
a difference in other people's lives—
things like love, compassion, and kindness.

CHALLENGE

List ways that you could remember to put on God's kind of clothes the next time you get dressed. Could you hang a card with Colossians 3:12 printed on it on your mirror? Could you draw something and put it on your closet that will help you remember?

Dare!

. . .TO TELL THE TRUTH

A lying tongue hates those it crushes,
and a mouth that speaks false words destroys.

PROVERBS 26:28

Telling the truth and being a trustworthy person means that you are honest and you do what you say you're going to do. This is also called "keeping your word." When you keep your word, people trust you and feel like they can count on you. Ephesians 4:25 (MSG) says, "What this adds up to, then, is this: no more lies, no more pretense. Tell your neighbor the truth. In Christ's body we're all connected to each other, after all. When you lie to others, you end up lying to yourself."

....

....

....

....

....

....

....

....

....

Jesus, I want to be trustworthy.
Help me always to keep my word.

CHALLENGE

Ask God to show you the fruit of telling the truth and being an honest person. Telling the truth brings good fruit. That means that good things happen when you tell the truth—you're known as an honest person, your parents and friends trust you, you get more privileges and responsibilities because you are trusted, and more. Write down what you hear from God about the fruit of telling the truth.

Dare!

...TO HEAR FROM GOD

Long ago God spoke to our early fathers in many different ways. He spoke through the early preachers. But in these last days He has spoken to us through His Son. God gave His Son everything. It was by His Son that God made the world.

HEBREWS 1:1–2

Through Jesus, God created and saved the world. Jesus is God in a perfect human body. When you look at Jesus, you get a clear picture of God. And He can speak directly to you. When you pray, make it a conversation where you talk a little and then listen a little. You may not hear an out-loud voice, but Jesus can speak to your heart as He answers your prayers and talks to you. And He will make Himself clear to you if you seek Him.

....

....

....

....

....

....

....

....

....

....

....

Jesus, thanks for wanting to talk to me! Help me to be able to hear from You and get to know Your voice.

CHALLENGE

In Jeremiah 29:13 (NIV), God says, "You will seek me and find me when you seek me with all your heart." Ask Jesus to speak clearly to you today. What is He saying? Journal anything that God puts on your heart.

....

....

....

....

....

....

....

....

....

....

....

....

Dare!

. . .TO THINK LIKE JESUS

Jesus knew what they were thinking. He said,
"Why do you think bad thoughts in your hearts?"

Matthew 9:4

The things you think about are important to Jesus. That's because your thoughts affect everything you do and say. Jesus wants His followers to stop hurting each other and having bad thoughts. But you can't do this on your own. You need supernatural help from the Holy Spirit. Jesus wants to help you become more like Him, and He is always ready to help you stop thinking bad thoughts and turn your attention to Him instead.

....

....

....

....

....

....

....

....

....

....

....

Lord, I want to think good things about You and other people.
Please help me become more like You.

CHALLENGE

Look up these verses: Ephesians 4:31–32 and Philippians 4:8. What do these scriptures tell us about our thoughts?

Dare!

...TO LOOK OUTSIDE THE BOX

*God is able to do much more than we ask
or think through His power working in us.*

EPHESIANS 3:20

When God's power is at work within you, the possibilities are beyond your imagination.

Remember that things aren't always what they seem. If you feel disappointed in God's answers to your prayers, look outside the box. God is always, always working everything out for your good (Romans 8:28). God sees the end from the beginning. What may have felt like the best answer may have been very bad for you or someone you love. Trust that God can do much more than anything you could ever ask or imagine!

Lord, help me to trust that You are working
everything out in the best possible way.

CHALLENGE

List some problems you are having right now. Whatever issue you are facing—big or small—God cares. As you pray and think about it, don't put God in a box, thinking that there is no way out or that there is only one right answer. His response just might be beyond your understanding and your wildest imagination. Bring each issue to Him in prayer. Place a check mark or a star by each problem after you have prayed and chosen to leave the outcome to God.

. . .TO SHOW GRACE

Live and work without pride. Be gentle and kind. Do not be hard on others. Let love keep you from doing that.

Ephesians 4:2

There is always a reason for why people act the way they do, even if they don't know it themselves. But God knows! That's why you should pray for the people who bother you. Your prayers can help change their hearts—and yours in the process too! You can have lots of grace for others because of God's love living inside you.

....

....

....

....

....

....

....

....

....

....

God, I don't always understand why people act the way they do, but I pray You would fill me with Your grace and love for them.

CHALLENGE

Think of someone in your life who bothers you. Ask Jesus to help you understand why they act the way they do. How can you show more grace to that person? (Remember, though, someone who is regularly bullying or hurting you physically needs to be reported to a trusted grown-up right away. Talk to your parents about what this means.)

....

....

....

....

....

....

....

....

....

....

Dare!

...TO BE STRONG

"Have I not told you? Be strong and have strength of heart! Do not be afraid or lose faith. For the Lord your God is with you anywhere you go."

Joshua 1:9

If you've trusted Christ as your Savior, the Spirit of God Himself is alive and well and working inside you at all times. What an astounding miracle! The Creator of the universe dwells within you and is available to encourage you and help you make good choices in every moment. Be encouraged! Even when it might feel like it, you are truly never alone. You always have access to God's power. God wants you to be strong and brave, relying on His power.

....

....

....

....

....

....

....

....

....

....

....

Lord, help me to be strong and brave, knowing
that my courage and strength come from You.

CHALLENGE

Write down anything that is troubling you or causing fear. God wants you to talk with Him about every little thing. Trust that God Himself will never leave you and that He is working everything out. Ask Jesus for help trusting Him. What does He want you to know about your problem?

Dare!

...TO TURN OFF ANGER

A gentle answer turns away anger,
but a sharp word causes anger.

PROVERBS 15:1

Have you ever been in an argument with a sibling or a friend? Both of you want to be right about whatever is happening. But instead of stirring up someone else's anger, Jesus tells us to answer with gentleness. By answering someone with gentleness, you can turn off their anger and end the argument. And if that doesn't work, you can just walk away until you both have calmed down.

....

....

....

....

....

....

....

....

....

....

....

God, help me to be strong and gentle at the same time. Please give me Your strength as I face anyone who may be angry in the future. Help me to answer gently or to walk away.

CHALLENGE

Proverbs 29:11 in the New International Version says, "Fools give full vent to their rage, but the wise bring calm in the end." Write it in your own words. Then ask Jesus to help you with your anger. Commit to go to Him first before getting in an argument.

Dare!

...TO CHOOSE LIFE

"I call heaven and earth to speak against you today. I have put in front of you life and death, the good and the curse. So choose life so you and your children after you may live. Love the Lord your God and obey His voice. Hold on to Him. For He is your life, and by Him your days will be long."

Deuteronomy 30:19–20

You have a choice every day of your life to follow Jesus and stay close to Him—or not. Life with Jesus is the most amazing adventure you can ever go on. The Bible says that eternal life is knowing God through His Son, Jesus Christ (John 17:3), and that Jesus came to give us abundant life (John 10:10)—even here, right now on this earth. You don't have to wait for heaven to experience this abundant-life adventure. It starts now!

....

....

....

....

....

....

....

....

....

....

Thank You for giving me life, Jesus. Help me
stay close to You all the days of my life.

CHALLENGE

Choosing Jesus won't always be easy. Some days it will be downright hard. But it is always worth it. Journal about a time when it was difficult to choose Jesus during a certain situation. What happened? Can you look back and see God at work in that situation?

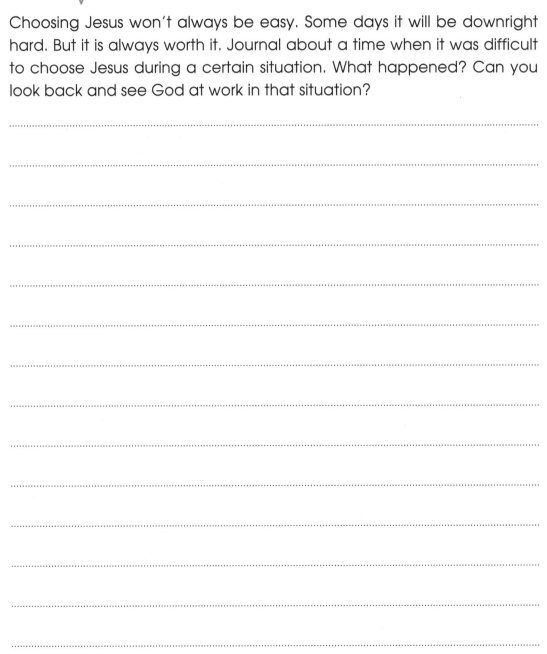

Dare!

. . .TO JUST BE YOU

Everything God made is good. We should not put anything aside if we can take it and thank God for it.

1 Timothy 4:4

God created you, and everything He created is good. You might wish you were more outgoing like some of your friends or that you looked a little different, but God created you exactly the way He wanted you to be. Your personality is the way God made you, and He wants to use that for His glory. He gave you the body you have for a reason, so take good care of it and thank Him for it.

....

....

....

....

....

....

....

....

....

....

....

God, please change my heart to match Yours. Help me to believe that what You say is true. Help me to be myself—just the way You made me.

CHALLENGE

Look at yourself in the mirror. Journal what you think about as you look at yourself. Now ask God to help you see yourself as He sees you. Journal what you see now.

. . .TO BE LIKE JESUS

"But love those who hate you. Do good to them. Let them use your things and do not expect something back. Your reward will be much. You will be the children of the Most High. He is kind to those who are not thankful and to those who are full of sin."

Luke 6:35

You might not have many enemies yet, but you will come across a lot of people in your lifetime who don't like Christians. People who are angry at Christians have usually been wounded deeply by other people pretending to be Christians. They think that God is just like the Christians who have hurt them. They've believed a lie about God. Knowing and remembering this can help us love them even when they don't act very lovable.

....

....

....

....

....

....

....

....

....

....

....

....

Jesus, help me to see others as You see them. Help me to be kind to people who are unkind so that they can know what You are really like.

CHALLENGE

Do you know anyone who doesn't like Christians? Write down that person's name, and ask God to show them the truth of who He is. Pray that God will soften their heart and become real to them. Pray that their wounded heart will be healed.

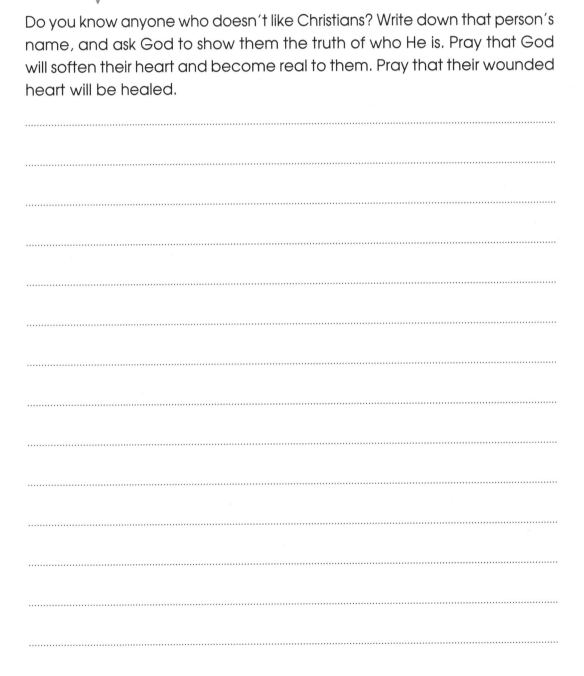

Dare!

...TO NOT COMPARE

We do not compare ourselves with those who think they are good. They compare themselves with themselves. They decide what they think is good or bad and compare themselves with those ideas. They are foolish.

2 Corinthians 10:12

When you compare yourself to others, you either start to feel prideful (like you're better than others), or you get very insecure (like you're not as good as others). But God made you unique on purpose. You are awesome just the way you are. It's who you are on the inside that matters to God. He made you on purpose for a purpose. The way you look and the gifts and talents you have can all be used by God. He has great plans for your life.

God, please forgive me for comparing myself to others.
Help me to be content with just the way You made me.

CHALLENGE

Journal about ways you've compared yourself to others in the past. How did comparing make you feel? What does God want you to do instead?

Dare!

...TO KNOW YOUR PURPOSE

Jesus said to him, " 'You must love the Lord your God with all your heart and with all your soul and with all your mind.' This is the first and greatest of the Laws. The second is like it, 'You must love your neighbor as you love yourself.' All the Laws and the writings of the early preachers depend on these two most important Laws."

MATTHEW 22:37–40

God made His purpose to His followers very clear: He wants us to love Him and love others. That sums up *everything* the Bible is trying to teach us. If we're just following rules, we've missed the whole point. Remember, God *is* love. Everything He does is done because of love. That's what He wants from us too. He wants us to obey Him because of love, to serve Him because of love, to worship Him because of love, to be kind to our neighbors because of love.

....

....

....

....

....

....

....

....

....

....

Thank You for making my purpose easy to understand, Jesus. I love You. I'll do my best to love others too—with Your help!

CHALLENGE

Look up 1 John 4:19. If our purpose is love, where does our capacity to love come from? How does this help us with our purpose? Journal your thoughts.

_____

_____

_____

_____

_____

_____

_____

_____

_____

_____

_____

Dare!

. . .TO ADVENTURE WITH JESUS

Jesus said, "Come!" Peter got out of the boat and walked on the water to Jesus. But when he saw the strong wind, he was afraid. He began to go down in the water. He cried out, "Lord, save me!"

Matthew 14:29–30

Jesus loves a good adventure. In fact, one time He called His friend Peter to get out of a boat and walk on top of the water. Can you imagine that? Peter jumped right out of that boat and thought it was really cool. But then He took His eyes off Jesus and started looking around. What do you think happened next? Yep, Peter realized what he was actually doing, and he got scared. Then he started to sink! What does this true story tell you? It's easy to get scared really quick when you take your eyes off Jesus.

....

....

....

....

....

....

....

....

....

....

Help me always to keep my eyes on You, Jesus.

CHALLENGE

You'll probably have some scary things happen to you as you grow up.
But you don't have to live in fear. Look up Matthew 14:27. Write down
what Jesus has to say to you.

....

....

....

....

....

....

....

....

....

....

. . .TO FOLLOW JESUS

Jesus said to His followers, "If anyone wants to be My follower, he must forget about himself. He must take up his cross and follow Me."

Matthew 16:24

Jesus tells us that to be His follower, we need to put God's plans for us before our own plans. We need to trust God to take care of us, because His ways are always higher than our own ways. He knows what's best for us. Back in Bible times, following Jesus was a dangerous thing to do. The disciples risked everything to follow Jesus, and the kingdom of God has spread to all the nations because of it.

....

....

....

....

....

....

....

....

....

....

....

Jesus, please give me the courage to help grow Your kingdom by sharing my faith with others. I trust You to take care of me!

CHALLENGE

What is Jesus asking you to do to help grow His kingdom? If Jesus' disciples trusted Jesus with their lives, can you trust Jesus to help you share His love with a friend in need? Ask Him to give you the kind of faith where you trust Jesus for everything—your food, your safety, your very life. Journal your prayer to God here.